Words into Elephants

Tiny Poems

Nolcha Fox

Words into Elephants - Tiny Poems

All poems are © Nolcha Fox

ISBN 978-1-962374-27-9 Paperback
ISBN 978-1-962374-28-6 EBook

Published by Prolific Pulse Press LLC
Raleigh, North Carolina USA

August 2024

Library of Congress Control Number: 2024913618

Table of Contents

Acknowledgments.. vii

A broken promise..1

A car passes on a rainy street 2

A swerve 3

A Tidy Life 4

After the lies...5

After the rain 6

At precisely the time 7

Baubles and Bubbles...8

Belts in the Sky 9

Bird Brain...10

Borderline 11

Breakfast 12

Broken Wheels...13

Buzzz..14

Canned Fruit Salad..15

Chicken, Chicken, Chicken...16

Colors Are Running 17

Coordinated..18

Dirty Clothes..19

Dogs and buttered toast aren't cats 20

Dogs on Drugs 21

Don't 22

Fragments...23

Fuzzy dust bunnies..24

Get Lost..25

Glow worms glisten 26

Happiness is an elephant 27

He can bearly make it 28

Higher Education 29

Holy Dementia 30

I asked the birds 31

I Can't Sing Loud Enough 32

I have big dreams 33

I stuffed my anger 34

I swim in a sea..35

I Would Rather...36

If I am what 37

In the Toilet..38

Innocents 39

Inverted 40

Invisible...41

It Is What It Is 42

Lean on Me 43

Let me endure 44

Lights sparkle outside 45

Marshmallow Mouth 46

Masks 47

Maze 48

Missed Landing...49

Moonlight and Shadows 50

Morgan le Fey 51

Morning is a river..52

Morning Rain Forgiven.................................53

Murder for Hire....................................54

My muse...55

My shovel...56

No Bluebirds Here 57

Photosynthesis....................................58

Pizza Gene 59

Pocket Cake 60

Pumpkin 61

Rain 62

Reflection 63

Sad Seagull.......................................64

She opened her heart 65

She's an alley cat 66

Silent Treatment..................................67

Smooth Operator...................................68

Soft white bread 69

Sticky Kisses.....................................70

Sunny Side 71

Tambourine 72

Temple 73

The Big Bounce 74

The Darkness 75

The Morning Is Too Loud...........................76

Today is as exciting 77

Trust 78

What a Shame 79

What's so smart 80

When the tide 81

Which? 82

Why I Can't Find My Father 83

Wild Parade 84

Words into Elephants 85

You 86

Your cigar is missing 87

About the Author 88

Credits for Art and Photographs 90

Acknowledgments

I started this book to capture all my micro-poetry (10 lines or less, including the title, excluding spaces) as these little poems flew out of my brain into literary magazines.

Many were written from prompts provided during April 2022 National Poetry Month. Thanks to the many poets who provided these prompts, they have no idea what they started.

Thanks to these literary magazines for publishing my poems:

- *Alien Buddha Zine*: "Borderline," "Temple," "Trust," "It Is What It Is"
- *Aurora Journal*: "Photosynthesis"
- *Dark Entries*: "A Tidy Life," "The Darkness," "What a Shame," "Why I Can't Find My Father," "Your Cigar Is Missing"
- *Dark Winter*: "Canned Fruit Salad"
- *Diphthong Lit*: "Breakfast"
- *Entropy*: "A Tidy Life," "The Darkness," "Why I Can't Find My Father," "Your Cigar is Missing"
- *Five Fleas*: "In the Toilet, "Invisible," "My muse," "Rain"
- *Lothlorien Poetry Journal*: "At precisely the time," "Moonlight and Shadows," "Morgan le Fey"
- *MasticadoresUsa*: "Happiness is an elephant"
- *Medusa's Kitchen*: "A car passes on a rainy street," "A swerve," "After the rain," "Baubles and Bubbles," "Bird Brain," "Broken Wheels," "Buzzz," "Chicken, Chicken, Chicken," "Colors Are Running," "Coordinated," "Dirty Clothes," "Dogs and

buttered toast aren't cats" "Dogs on Drugs," "Don't," "Fuzzy dust bunnies," "Get Lost," "Glow worms glisten," "He can bearly make it," "I Can't Sing Loud Enough," "I have big dreams," "I stuffed my anger," "I swim in a sea," "If I am what," "Innocents," "Lights sparkle outside," "Marshmallow Mouth," "Masks," "Maze," "Missed Landing," "Morning Rain Forgiven," "Murder for Hire," "My shovel," "No Bluebirds Here," "Pizza Gene," "She opened her heart," "She's an alley cat," "Smooth Operator," "Soft white bread," "Sticky Kisses," "Sunny Side," "The Big Bounce," "The Morning Is Too Loud," "Today is as exciting," "What's so smart," "Which?" "You"

- *Poetry Life and Times*: "Higher Education," "Holy Dementia"
- *Spillwords*: "Lean on Me"
- Sweetycat Press ZOOANTHOLOGY: "Sad Seagull"
- *The Piker Press*: "After the lies," "I Would Rather"
- *The Writers Club*: "I asked the birds," "Let me endure," "Morning is a river," "Words into Elephants"
- *Whispers and Echoes*: "Belts in the Sky," "Dogs and buttered toast aren't cats" "Inverted," "Pocket Cake," "Wild Parade"
- *WyoPoets News*: "Pumpkin"

Thanks to Sarah, Tony, and Tom for reading first drafts and cheering me on.

Thanks to my family, who made me what I am.

A broken promise

can't be fixed.
No glue can put it
back together.
Its shards are scattered
in dark alleys,
buried under good intentions,
thrown into the trash.

A car passes on a rainy street

and it's not you.
Headlights
are owl's eyes
blinking through
shimmering waterfalls.
Windshield wipers
can't swim against
this downpour
of tears.

A swerve

around a bug-eyed doe,
I crash into the guardrail.
The tire flat, the hub cap bent.
I don't think first to call for help.
I recall the cake I baked.
It looked just like that tire.

A Tidy Life

You strangle what you can't control.
No living thing survives your grip.
Your life is draped in plastic.
No dust, no germs, no guests
allowed to linger.
No sloppy feelings interfere
with your well-oiled plans.

So remote, you won't be missed.
Your death will not be noticed.

After the lies

I believed in are gone,
all that is left
is the last laugh
of destiny,
musty midnight
transgressions
baked into
my bones.

After the rain

the air we breathe
is a peppermint
kiss on the cheek.

At precisely the time

the world ends,
my attention wanders
to the brick of light
through the window
chasing deadbeat
shadows and blank spaces.

Baubles and Bubbles

She was spare change
wasted on shiny baubles,
spare time drowned
in bubble baths,
passing fancy food,
leaving nothing
but empty pockets,
a bathtub ring,
and indigestion.

Belts in the Sky

You say if I look carefully,
I'll see belts, the buckles gleaming
in the evening sky.
Do you mean the asteroid belts?
And heavens, did they lose their pants?

Bird Brain

My head is just a bird cage,
my life is a dead bird.
My recollections
are collections
of bird turds
that the ceiling fan
wooshes away.

Borderline

I straddle the borderline
between what I sense
and what makes no sense.
I call this place nonsense.
If that makes sense.

Breakfast

is a bowl
of chronic
stress,
full of
pebbles
looking
for a shoe.

Broken Wheels

The motorcycle,
the lawn mower,
crumble into rust,
forgotten by
dirt and grass,
abandoned by history,
by human touch.

Buzzz

I flit from diversion
to distraction,
fueled by caffeine
and adrenaline.
I'm so buzzed
I can talk to electricity.

Canned Fruit Salad

Cheap bastards.
Only one cherry.
The only thing
worth fighting for.

Now I'm going
to walk away and

gag at all that
sweet sludge.

Chicken, Chicken, Chicken

A black chicken,
frantic to return
to the other side,
ran along the fence.
I wanted to help her,
but she clucked
and fluffed away so fast,
she must have thought
I wanted hot wings.

Colors Are Running

Colors are running, rain on a painting.
They streak nude through the streets.
Rose, turquoise, purple, they reach up to moonlight,
they dance on the roof to the beat of the rain.
Purple stops at Mom's place to go through old
photos.
Turquoise grabs a latte, then leaps into bed.
Rose steals my car, then blows through a stop sign.
I get the ticket, and win a cigar.

Coordinated

I curtsy,
a cow on crutches,
crashing the conspiracy
of cults,
chewing cures
and contracts
into cud.

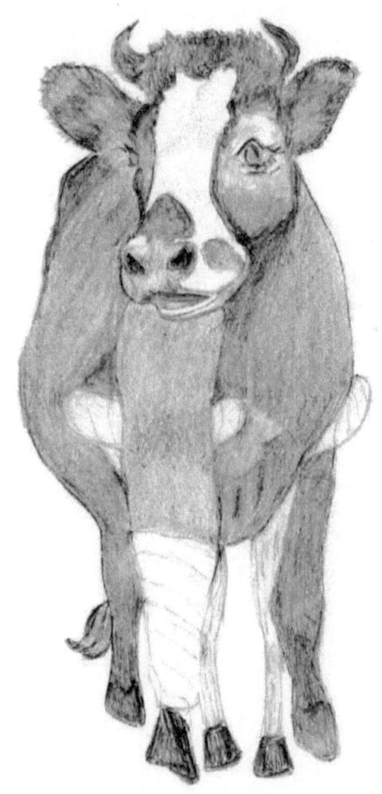

Dirty Clothes

If I lived on the Maine coast,
overlooking the ocean,
wash day would never come.
Instead of bending over,
washing dirty clothes,
I'd stand tall in my yard
and let the wind blow me away.

inspired by:
"Wash Day on the Maine Coast"
—Painting by N.C. Wyeth, 1934

Dogs and buttered toast aren't cats

because they land wrong side down.
You are a cat, elegant
in words, in motion.
I'm not fooled
by slick persuasion.
At heart you are
a dirty dog.
Your toast is buttered
with margarine.

Dogs on Drugs

Dogs
Rush in
Under, around my feet
Goo-goo eyes only for food
Spinning

Don't

touch the horn,
It's antique
like me
and it can break.
If you really
want to hear
the music,
pay full price

and toot your own horn.

Fragments

Sunrise pokes through
holes in lace curtains,
fragments of bright
in the shadows.

Sunrise reflects in
my ring's diamond facets,
fragments of bright
in the gloom.

Fuzzy dust bunnies

should be fuzzy ducklings.
They'd march out the door.
I wouldn't need
a broom and dustpan.

Get Lost

That's the way it's always been:
You say, "Tomato." I say, "Get lost."
If you were a fly, I'd swat you.
But you refuse to leave,
buzzing round my ears, a nuisance,
until I eat that ripe, red fruit
and you go out to garden.

Glow worms glisten

incandescent,
dangling orbs,
rippling reflections
in the rain,
a path to follow
home.

Happiness is an elephant

sitting in the best chair,
hogging the remote.
I can only feed him peanuts
and vacuum when he
goes to the refrigerator
for a beer.

He can bearly make it

through the day.
It's a tough job,
sprawled upon
the ground
to hold the earth
in orbit round the sun.

Higher Education

The mathematician
is training to work
at McDonalds.
Today he is learning
how to make ice cubed.

Holy Dementia
a response to Mary Ruefle, "On Twilight"

As he wanders
through his creation,
I wonder if God
picks me up
from another fall
and says,
"I made this?"

I asked the birds

if they wanted to be a poem.
They cocked their heads,
blessed me with one eye,
and seeing that I had
no food, no words,
they launched into the sky,
splitting the clouds
with their wings.

I Can't Sing Loud Enough

I can't sing loud enough
to shatter illusions,
to fracture denial.

I can't sing loud enough
to forgive the dead,
to give the living solace.

If I can't sing louder
so someone can hear me,
why should I sing at all?

I have big dreams

bigger than this
seashell
I hide in
from the sharks.
I'll upgrade
to a pickup truck
and camper shell,
hit the open road
and see the world.

I stuffed my anger

into a glass marble
and stuck it in my pocket.
When it cooled off,
I buried that marble
in the garden.
I wait for it to grow
into a flower.

I swim in a sea

of strangers,
waves of
joy crashing
in this
crowded room.

I Would Rather

I would rather drink the clouds,
hear the roses sing to rivers,
taste the leaves before they fall,
smell the twilight,
laugh at darkness,
free the wild child in my heart,

than watch my image in the mirror
glowing dimmer,
fading into gold.

If I am what

I drink,
I am a jar
of instant espresso.

In the Toilet

I found a spaceship
in the toilet,
floating with a deck
of cards.
I laid them all out
on the couch
then dried them with
this poem.

Innocents

We kill what we
cannot control.
We rage against
the ones who can't
fight back.
In the massacre
of innocents,
we slaughter
our innocence, too.

Inverted

In the mirror
world inverted,
where left is right,
right is left.
Does time run backward
behind the glass?

Invisible

You don't see me.
My face is scuffed.
Ignored again.
A stray post-it.
A scribble stuck to the floor.
Trod upon.
Faded ink.
Faded life.

It Is What It Is

Is your kiss invitation or a snare?
I don't know. It is what it is.

You say you want me. You don't say for what.
How can I trust you? It is what it is.

Come with me, you say, let's go somewhere new.
I can't decide. It is what it is.

You throw up your hands and walk out the door.
I'm better alone. It is what it is.

Lean on Me

I am the cane that steadies you.
I am the solid wall
that keeps your chair from tipping.
When you feel abandoned,
I am your last friend.
Trust me, I'm always here for you.
Isn't that what anger is for?

Let me endure

the blinding light that
scorches my skin,
combusts the cracks
between my bones,
bonfires my brain,
eats my eyes,
turns me into gold.

Lights sparkle outside

the window,
dancing firework
fallout surfing
midnight wind.
Are they lost
fireflies,
sparks from a blaze,
or dragon dust
from another land?

Marshmallow Mouth

Words wobble off your tongue,
gooshy, mooshy sweet white,
pregnant with potential
left unsaid, best guessed,
S'mores in desire's fire.

Masks

We put our masks on
every morning,
masks that smile,
masks that show we care.
Underneath we yawn,
we crossword puzzle.
Underneath we couldn't
give a hoot.

Maze

We're stuck in leafy maze
of our design.
Sticking heads into
the hedges, looking
to escape each other,
stalking clues
to secret exits.

Missed Landing

She flies in circles round the yard,
a kamikaze, reckless abandon.
A final leap, she hits the landing
with her chin.
A body shake later, she prances in,
proud that she hit the target.

Moonlight and Shadows

The moon is a narcotic,
a dose of dreams.
We stagger under its weight,
resting only in shadows
of trees and walls.

Morgan le Fey

Your robes and cape
are partners to your dance,
a swirl of filmy, floating
colored gauze.
As you raise the magic
glowing in your hand,
you are a sorceress
spider spinning webs
of treachery and death.

Morning is a river

he struggles to cross,
leaning against loss,
stumbling on stones
of a life of almost
but not quite,
sinking into sand filled
with metal findings,
enough to build a cage
without a door.

Morning Rain Forgiven

I forgive the tears
that slide down my window,
rivulets of snail trails
that sparkle in the morning sun,
to gather on the sill.
Is it me or someone else
who cries?

Murder for Hire

I hired free verse
to kill every poetic form
within a stanza's radius.

The judge didn't care
I was strangled by rules.
He sentenced me to
death by sonnet.

My muse

is gone, she left a note
that she went shopping
with the girls.
I hope I didn't send her
on another bender.
My writing might be much worse
than I think.

My shovel

turned blue
from digging a hole
in the sky.

No Bluebirds Here
Response poem to "Bluebirds" by Charles Bukowski

Once I had
a bluebird in my heart,
until it crapped all over the place,
and left insect parts on the floor
for the cat to eat.
I let that bluebird out,
and I haven't been sorry since.

Photosynthesis

Under fairy lights,
asters germinate together,
a photosynthesis
to empty sour sorrow
into milk bread,
to dissolve aster leaves
into sweet tea
serenity.
Let healing overflow.

Pizza Gene

Gene lives for
take-out pizza,
ultra-vegetarian.
Cheese and sauce,
no pepperoni,
anchovies
mushrooms,
onions, olives.
Only extra-large.

Pocket Cake

Cake in my pocket
to feed the squirrels
in the college square.
Free food,
free tuition,
squirrels are much smarter
than me.

Pumpkin

Your sweetness is consumed.
You are a hollow, knobby shell
of what you used to be.
Toothless, you bellow
of children dressed as nightmares,
who kicked you to
a rocky resting place.
Your anger is the opposite
of your faded orange skin.

Rain

Rain on the walkway.
Dogs with no
wish for wet.
No sun.
No play.
Dogs on the couch
until dinner.

Reflection

She looked at herself in the mirror.
Her face shattered.

Sad Seagull

Cries shatter the sun,
wings slice the air,
sad seagull.
Sky shards fall and pierce
the sand in your wake.
You don't want to leave,
you don't want to stay.
Fly me on your back
across the ocean.

She opened her heart

and the bluebird of happiness
flew inside.
Now she's so stuffed
with bird poop
and bird seed,
she can't zip up
her pants.

She'd rather be thin
and depressed.

She's an alley cat

at midnight,
a first flight
of firelight,
prowling
the fish pond
in moonlight,
looking for
an easy catch.

Silent Treatment

Silence is stalking
the run in my stocking,
my fashion is shocking,
they all turn away.

Smooth Operator

Ladies, don't believe him.
Don't trust his sweet words.
They melt in his mouth,
but they'll freeze your brain.
By the time you defrost your senses,
he'll have stolen your heart
and your purse.

Soft white bread

folds and trembles
when weighted
down with
meat and cheese.
But it's great
for squeezing
into balls to
throw at other people.

Sticky Kisses

We share some chocolate,
and then a sticky kiss.
Your lips
a sweet delight.

The dog jumps
between us,
covers our faces
with sticky kisses.

I think she got into the chocolate.

Sunny Side
from "On the Sunny Side of the Street" by Jimmy McHugh

My lips are sealed,
but I'm all ears.
Tell me all your secrets
on the sunny side of discreet.

Tambourine

A secret passageway to song,
primeval dance around the fire.
We jump and sway, uncivilized,
a savage heat revealing.
Suspended on the borderline
between nightfall and bright,
we're in a trance, a tribal glow,
brought on by tambourine.

Temple

This migraine is a hammer
and chisel to my right temple,
a right temple wronged,
temple stones teetering,
temple columns collapsing into dust.
Monks, nuns, and priests
run out of my temple,
praying as they dodge
the falling rocks.

The Big Bounce

He bounces up and down,
trying every mattress
in the store.
The last bed bounce
throws him up,
and he never
comes
down.

The Darkness

The darkness follows me home.
The darkness makes peanut brittle in my microwave.
The darkness makes a nest in my hair.
The darkness weeds my garden.
The darkness sits next to me at the bar, drinking
wine.
The darkness is the wine.

The Morning Is Too Loud

The morning swings a hammer, shatters darkness.
The morning pulses peonies and primrose.
The morning strips my stupor to the Rolling Stones.
The morning clatters pots and pans.
The morning barks at deer across the street.
I want to tie the morning up, slap duct tape on its
mouth.

Today is as exciting

as sliced white bread
with no butter,
no honey,
a day looking
forward to becoming
a rancid tuna salad
sandwich.

Trust

Trust is a broken watch,
parched flowers
dropping wilted
petals on the table.

Trust is fashionably late
one time too many,
an exquisite corpse stuffed
in an empty suitcase.

What a Shame

I saved shame as pebbles.
I hide them in my shoes.
Tiny, but irritating.

I saved shame as arrowheads.
I hide them in my shoulder hunch.
Otherwise, they pierce.

I saved shame as daggers.
I hide them in my tongue.
Talking is deadly.

What's so smart

about a smartphone?
Mine was too dumb
to tell me
I was walking
in front

of a bus.

When the tide

washes away
the sands of time,
does the world begin again?

Or does it end?

Which?

When right shoe fits
left foot, left shoe
fits right foot,
how do I walk
when feet switch sides?

Why I Can't Find My Father

I dig through snow
with frozen fingers.
Branches scratch
words in the sky.
Don't bother.
We touched
the ground
and stole
his grave.

Wild Parade

Cottonwoods line the street,
tossing white confetti
over wild turkeys strutting
in the middle of the road
to a marching band
only they hear.

Words into Elephants

The words
I blurt out
crush the couch,
suck up air
as you strangle,
eat the peanuts,
crack the floor,
as they lumber
out the door.

You

are a midnight black sky,
a seeping wound,
your eyes windows of despair,
shuttered to all hope,
your breath a trail of smoke
you follow to the plastic
bag over your head,
to the last exit
of your deserted road.

Your cigar is missing

from your grave.
Did you want
to fool the woman
recently buried
next to you?
Let her find out later
you like to smoke,
when she can't
get away.

About the Author

Life got interesting early on, starting with an escape in front of a hurricane to get out of town. This sense of the absurd planted the writing bug Nolcha expressed as wall art and margin doodles as a toddler. Writing eventually became a career and a passion.

Nolcha Fox's poems have been curated in print and online journals. Her poetry books are available on Amazon and Dancing Girl Press. Nominee for 2023 Best of The Net, 2024 Best of the Net Anthology. Nominee for a 2023 Pushcart Prize. Visual Editor for Chewers by Masticadores.

Websites:

bit.ly/3bT9tYu and nolchafox2.wixsite.com/nolcha-s-written-wor/blog

LinkedIn: linkedin.com/in/nolchafox/

Facebook: facebook.com/nolcha.fox/

Medium: @nolchafox_14571

Substack: @nolchafox

Credits for Art and Photographs

"Coordinated" and "Happiness is an elephant" drawings by Lisa Tomey-Zonneveld All rights reserved.

"He can bearly make it" - Unsplash

All other photographs and pictures are copyright protected.